Milton the Burl

Fulton Books
Meadville, PA

Published by Fulton Books 2022

ISBN 979-8-88505-305-1 (paperback)
ISBN 979-8-88505-307-5 (digital)

Printed in the United States of America

Milton the Burl

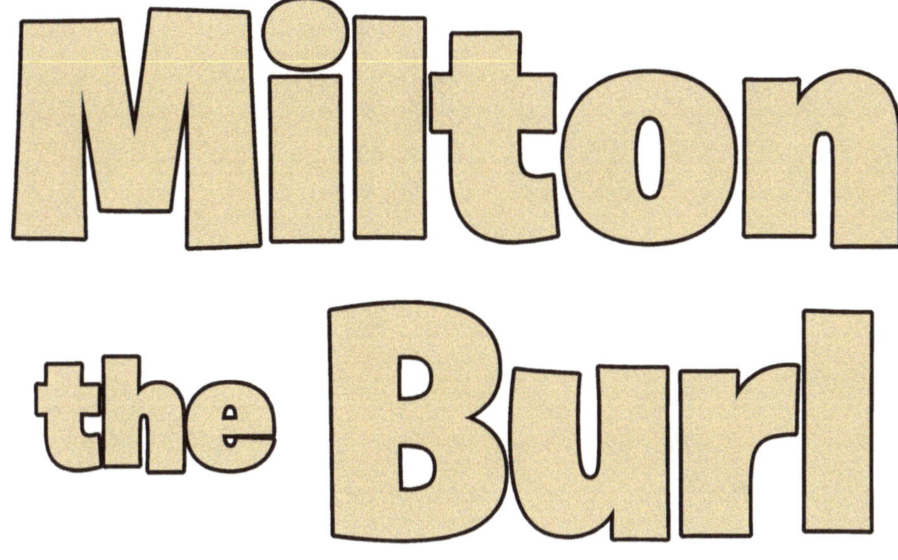

Marie Londonbridge

This is Milton. He's a burl.

He was once the base of the scrawniest tree in the forest. As the other trees around him grew bigger and taller, he grew wider and rounder, into a burl.

Milton is part of a white oak tree. Milton's tree had beautiful leaves and bark. No two trees are alike, but Milton the burl is really special.

One day, the farm where Milton lived turned into a housing community. Most of the trees were cut down to make way for the roads and houses, but not Milton. He and a few of the other trees got to remain.

The trees still surrounding him continued to grow taller and wider, but he just kept growing wider and wider.

Jessica and Mike loved having Milton in the yard where they lived. Families taking walks around the neighborhood would get a glimpse of Milton from the street, stopping by to take a closer look. The neighborhood kids thought Milton was really cool, and they marveled at the size of him, even though he looked so strange. They admired him and climbed on him. Milton was like a funny, natural jungle gym!

Milton was the talk of the neighborhood because he was so unusual.

One of the trees around Milton was a huge red oak tree. The red oak was very tall, big, and beautiful, with lots of full branches. The two trees could really drink some water when it was hot. Their roots went deep and wide and drank so much water the grass would turn brown in the summer. There wasn't enough rainwater for the grass and the two of them to drink. They were so big and so thirsty!

Milton's tree was special in a different way than the other trees around him. Milton started as a small tree and looked just like the others. It might have been due to something that got stuck in his trunk like a rock, or bugs, or an early tree sickness that made him grow the way he did. Maybe Milton knew why, but it didn't really matter. Sometimes Milton thought he wasn't as good-looking as the other trees, but he turned out to be the most special tree in the whole neighborhood. Milton was magnificent in a peculiar kind of way.

It wasn't just that he looked cool either. The way he grew was practical. Many other trees in the neighborhood grew too big to be around the houses. When a storm would come, some of their tree branches would fall onto roofs, or even become uprooted, which could be dangerous. Those trees had to be cut down. Sometimes they could be used for firewood to heat houses or toasty campfires. Other times they would just be taken to the dump or left in the yards, maybe to serve as an occasional seat for rabbits or a place for the squirrels to crack their nuts, but not really serving a purpose.

Milton was too special to be used in an ordinary way.

One day it came time to cut Milton's tree down. The owners were disappointed, but reluctantly called the tree cutters. They searched for a place where Milton the Burl could go once his tree was cut down. They called many tree cutters, but they all said they would just take Milton to the dump. The wood from Milton's tree and limbs could be used for firewood, but the tree cutters were not interested in finding a special use for Milton the Burl.

When the day came for Milton's tree to be cut down, one of the tree cutters, Ashton, saw Milton and was fascinated. He saw how saddened the owners were to see Milton go and told them he had a friend who had a sawmill. The sawmill is where trees go to be cut into lumber for building or for making furniture. Ashton said his friend might be interested in making Milton into a table for the owners. When Milton heard this, he got very excited. He began to imagine moving inside, to be something beautiful and useful for the family, to be adorned with inspiring books, refreshing drinks on coasters, and maybe even a bouquet of flowers.

Ashton called his friend, Jake, and sent him a picture of Milton. Jake was awed. He had never seen a burl that big. Milton might even be able to become more than one table!

The kids and neighbors stopped by to see Milton's tree being cut down and wanted to know what the owners were going to do with Milton. Once they found out Milton was going to the sawmill to be made into beautiful tables, that made them happy. Perhaps their parents would have a piece of Milton's burl in their house one day too.

On a warm spring day, Jake came by with a friend and some chain saws. Milton was so big the thirty-inch chain saw couldn't cut through him. They sawed and sawed. Milton even bent one of the chain saws. He couldn't help it! Smoke was pouring out of the hole in the top of Milton because of the heat coming from the saw. Milton's wood was so hard and thick Jake had to purchase an even-bigger chain saw. He bought one that was double in size, about sixty inches long. The new saw was taller than most of the neighborhood children!

Everyone had to wait for a couple of months for the new saw to be delivered. When it was, Jake came back and started sawing close to the base to keep as much of Milton as possible so he would be able to make several tables out of Milton's burl. At around 150 years old, some speculated that Milton was rotten or had metal inside of him to make him grow the way he did. But to everyone's surprise, Milton's base was solid and was only rotten in a tiny spot, which was normal for such an old burl. His wood inside was beautiful with all the tight tree rings that only filled a portion of Milton's burl because his tree was skinny compared to his burl.

Jake sawed and sawed until he could see that the saw went all the way through the burl to the other side.

Ashton called his friend, Conner, who had big equipment. They needed something huge to lift Milton off his base. Conner let Ashton borrow a big tractor called a front-end loader with big forks, and they pried Milton from his stump. When Milton came loose, the front of the loader went way up in the air on the back tires because Milton was so big and heavy. Finally, Milton was loose, and they lifted him onto Jakes trailer.

Once Milton was on the trailer, he had to be strapped down so he wouldn't fall off while traveling down the road to the sawmill. It was like a tree seat belt! The owners gave Milton a big hug and waved goodbye. The truck pulled out and down the road he went.

The owners already missed looking at the tree and Milton the Burl, as they had all those years in their yard. He was so special to see. But they knew they would see him again. Just in a slightly different form.

When Milton arrived at the sawmill, he needed to be cut into table sized slices. Milton was placed on a special saw that moved back and forth as it cut one slice at a time. The slabs, or slices, had to be cut at the right thickness for tables.

    Each piece had to be picked up using a tractor, called a skid loader, because they were so big and heavy.

After the pieces were cut, they needed to be dried or "cured." The fastest and best way was to place the wood slices in a kiln. The kiln's job is to heat up and add moisture to the air while fans blow on the wood to dry it out slowly so it won't crack apart. The slices of Milton that fit in the kiln would need to stay there for about a month. The other slices would need to dry out over time because they were too large to fit in the kiln. The slices were huge, ranging from four feet to eight feet around!

The owners stopped by the sawmill to see Milton and to choose which piece of his burl was the best size for them. The owners picked a nice piece they knew would be a perfect fit. They were excited to have Milton enjoy his next chapter as a table in their living room.

Once the pieces were dry, Milton was ready.

Mason the woodworker sanded the top and bottom to make sure it was nice and smooth. Then he filled in the cracks with a special material called epoxy. There were many colors to choose from, but the owners picked black.

The tabletop was finished, and now it needed a base. The owners found a steelmaker, Jose, who turns steel into railings, decorations, tables, or anything someone wants made. The design had to be just right for the heavy burl slice and had to match the owner's living room. Jose helped the owners pick just the right pieces and welded them together to make a beautiful table base.

The table base was then sent to a painter, who powder coated the steel to make it pretty and keep it from rusting. They picked a beautiful gold color. Powder coating is a special kind of spray paint that looks like powder and is then cured in an oven to make it stick. It looks great and lasts a long time, just like Milton.

After the table base was ready, the woodworkers drilled holes into the table base and underside of Milton's burl slice in just the right spots. Milton's slice was then secured to his base and now a complete table, a true masterpiece.

Finally, Milton's was ready to be picked up and brought back to Milton's home to be enjoyed for many years to come. He looked incredible.

The neighborhood kids still came to marvel at Milton. Jessica, Mike, and their friends played board games upon his surface, read books, and put drinks on coasters. So many wonderful gatherings, laughs, and memories are still made around Milton the Burl. Sometimes someone even brings him a bouquet of flowers. I wonder if anyone 150 years ago ever imagined that one day Milton the Burl would become such a spectacular sight for eyes to see.

The owners thought of Milton like an oyster that makes a pearl. When either sand or a tiny pebble gets inside it, something beautiful is made to last forever. Maybe you can take a walk in the woods or look out the window and find a burl while driving down the road one day. Trees have similarities to children. They are very special, unique in very different ways, and created by God for a good purpose.

About the Author

Marie Londonbridge comes from a long history of farmers. She grew up taking long walks with her father in the woods of southern Virginia on the family property. Her father would point out the different trees and taught Marie to identify them by their bark, leaves, and smell. She learned about nature, including beavers who made dams on their pond, birds, rabbits, deer, and snakes. She also learned about agriculture crops and field maintenance. Marie Londonbridge lives in a suburb outside of Washington, D. C., with her husband and family. She left corporate America to raise her daughter and become an entrepreneur. Marie dedicates much of her time volunteering, running a nonprofit food ministry focused on feeding seniors with her husband. (For more information about Milton the Burl, please email Marie at miltontheburl@aol.com.)

www.ingramcontent.com/pod-product-compliance
Lightning Source LLC
Chambersburg PA
CBHW041824110726
48006CB00019B/2494